Oxford University Press, Great Clarendon Street, Oxford OX2 6DP

Oxford New York
Athens Auckland Bangkok Bogotá
Buenos Aires Calcutta Cape Town Chennai
Dar es Salaam Delhi Florence Hong Kong
Istanbul Karachi Kuala Lumpur Madrid Melbourne
Mexico City Mumbai Nairobi Paris São Paolo
Singapore Taipei Tokyo Toronto Warsaw

and associated companies in
Berlin Ibadan

Oxford is a trade mark of Oxford University Press

Text copyright © John Butterworth 1994
Illustrations © Kate Sheppard 1994
First published 1994
Revised and updated 1998
5 7 9 10 8 6 4

ISBN 0-19-9104557

Typeset by Mike Brain, Oxford
Printed in Great Britain

Contents

Introduction

This is a book of activities and games to be used alongside *The Oxford Primary School Dictionary*. It will help you to understand dictionaries and to get the most out of them.

You can find a great wealth of information in a dictionary, if you know how to use it. But unless you are familiar with the way a dictionary works, it can seem more like a maze than a useful and helpful reference book. *Using the Oxford Primary School Dictionary* is a guide to help you explore the dictionary and to find your way around it.

The activities that follow will give you practice at looking up words and making sense of what the dictionary says about them. You will learn about the different kinds of English words, what they can do, and what they mean. You will also discover how words change to suit a number of different uses, and when it is right to use some words and wrong to use others.

This book also contains a number of quizzes and games where the answers are hidden in the dictionary, or where the dictionary is the 'referee'. Many of these are cross-curricular, which means that they belong not just to English, but to mathematics, music, geography, history, technology and science. Some others are based on everyday activities such as shopping, travelling and solving problems.

The tasks are fun to do, which is important, because language should be fun. Some may seem fairly easy, while others will be challenging and puzzling. Enjoy them and do them well; they will show you what a varied and fascinating book the dictionary is.

All in order

To help you find words in the dictionary, they are in alphabetical order.

a See how quickly you can find the following words. Time yourself.

tennis   volleyball   athletics   football   chess

b Can you find these in the dictionary?

1   a *fish* and a *bird* that begin with **her**

her ....

her ....

2   a unit of *time*, a unit of *length*, and a unit of *money* that all begin with **y**

y ....

y ....

y ....

3   a *motor vehicle* and a *boat* that begin with **tra**

tra ....

tra ....

c Put the following musical instruments into the order they come in the dictionary:

flute   ....

trumpet ....

piano   ....

guitar   ....

violin   ....

cello   ....

drum   ....

d Sort these animals into alphabetical order:

butterfly

....

boar

....

bird

....

bat

....

bear

....

bloodhound

....

e These words all begin with the same **two** letters. Put them into alphabetical order:

digger

....

dimmer

....

differ

....

dither

....

diver

....

f Rewrite these words in alphabetical order:

Mad mechanic Mick made monstrous mistakes mending motors.

....

....

....

Can you think of a silly sentence in which all the words begin with the same letter? Use the dictionary to help you.

....

....

Guides

To make it easier to find a word, most dictionaries have *guide* words at the top of their pages. In *The Oxford Primary School Dictionary*, they tell you the *first* and *last* words on each page.

a Look up the word **spot**. Which two guide words does it come between? Do the same for these words:

....   **stair**   ....

....   **roof**   ....

....   **ceiling**   ....

b Use the guide words to help you look up the names of these birds. Which two guide words do they come between?

....   **hawk**   ....

....   **sparrow**   ....

....   **vulture**   ....

c These are four guide words from the dictionary:

lifelong like		**like line**

Can you think of six or more words that would be on these two pages? Write them down.

....

....

....

Find these four guide words in *The Oxford Primary School Dictionary* and see how many words you could have written.

In Between

This is a game for two or more players and a referee who has the dictionary.

The referee chooses a double page from the dictionary and tells the players the guide words. For example:

cuff	currant	currency	cute

The players must *not* see the page.

The teams or players then have 5 minutes to write as many words as they can think of that would come between cuff and cutlass.

The referee calls 'time' and checks the answers.

Points: 1 for every right word
1 *off* for every wrong word.

Rule: Only the words in the dictionary that are printed in bold count towards the score.

Example guide words =
cuff, currency, current, cutlass

Guide words =

....

....

Example player or team 1		Blank score card	
Words	Points	Words	Points
custard ✓	+ 1		
cutter X	- 1		
curve ✓	+ 1		
cue X	- 1		

Entries

Each of the short sections in a dictionary is called an *entry*.

The entry begins with the *headword* in bold letters. The rest of the entry gives you information about the headword, or words related to it.

 Not all dictionary entries are the same length. Take the headwords:

brag and **break**

Try to guess which will have the bigger entry. Then look them up and see if you were right.

Can you see any other ways in which the two entries are different? For instance, which one has example sentences showing how the word is used?

 Look carefully at several different entries in your dictionary. Do you notice any kinds of information that *all* the entries have? List them.

 Here is a dictionary entry for the word **king**:

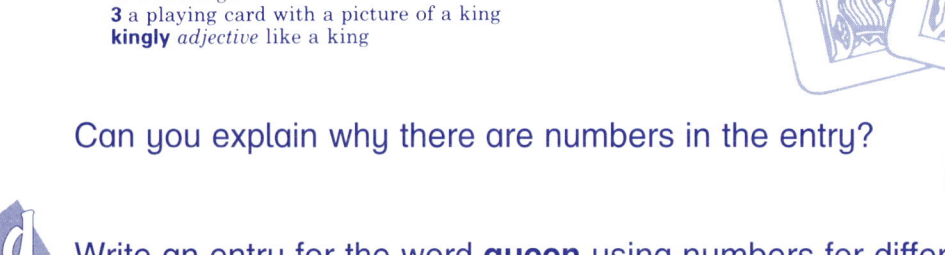

king *noun* (*plural* **kings**)
    1 a man who has been crowned as the ruler
    of a country
    2 a piece in chess that has to be captured
    to win the game
    3 a playing card with a picture of a king
    kingly *adjective* like a king

Can you explain why there are numbers in the entry?

 Write an entry for the word **queen** using numbers for different parts of the entry. Then compare your entry with the one for **queen** in the dictionary.

queen

....

....

....

....

....

....

....

Sometimes the headwords themselves have numbers after them:

bat[1] ➤ *noun* (*plural* **bats**)
    a wooden implement used to hit the ball in
    cricket, baseball, and other games
    off your own bat (*informal*) without any
    help from other people
bat ➤ *verb* (**bats**, **batting**, **batted**)
    to bat is to use a bat in a ball game
bat[2] *noun* (*plural* **bats**)
    a flying mammal that looks like a mouse
    with wings

Why do you think there is more than one entry for the word **bat**?

....

....

....

....

What's the meaning?

The main job of a dictionary is to tell us what words mean and to show us how they are spelt.

headword   meaning

clue noun (**clues**)
something that helps you solve a puzzle or a mystery.
not have a clue, to be ignorant or helpless.

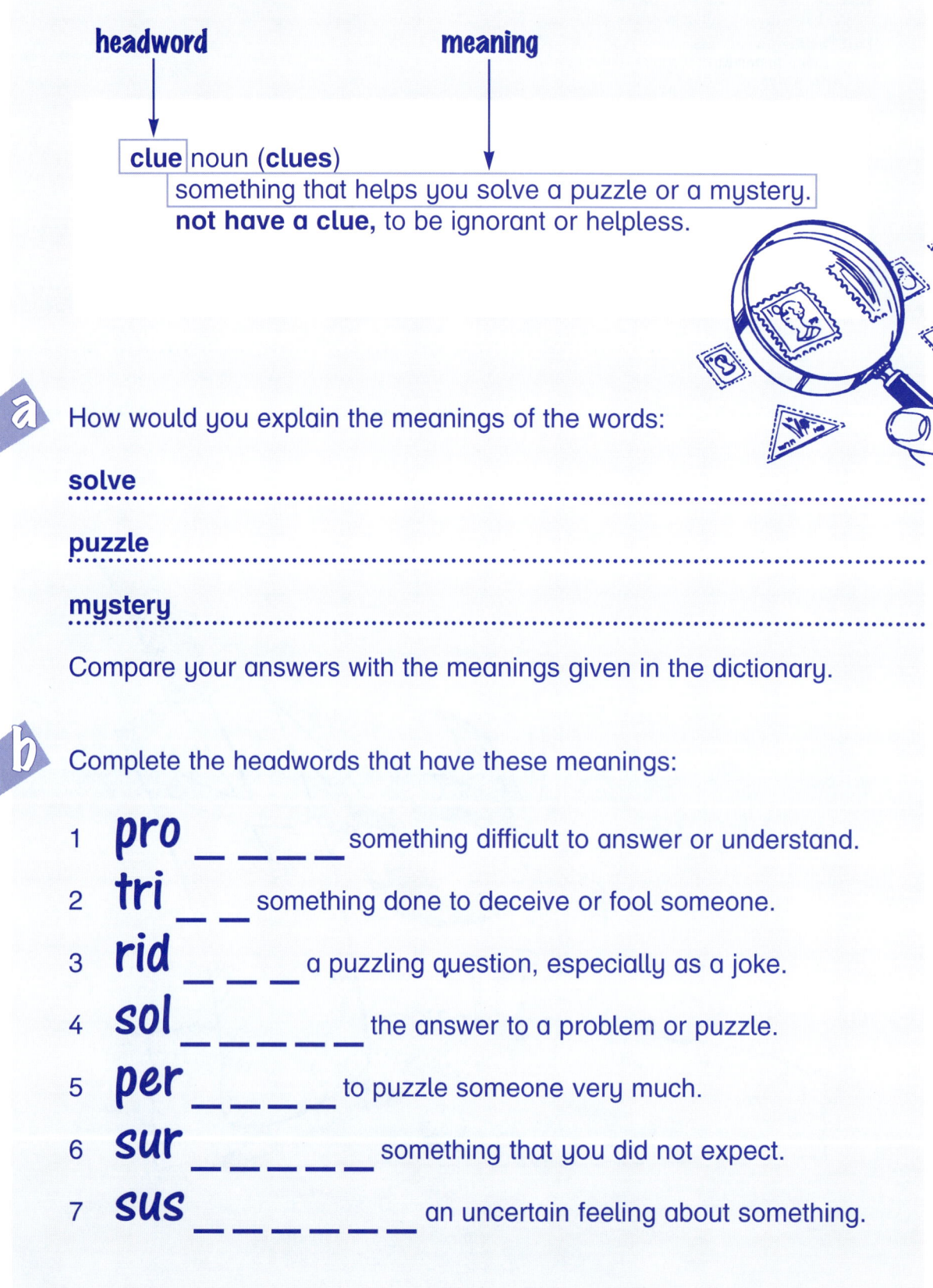

a How would you explain the meanings of the words:

solve ....

puzzle ....

mystery ....

Compare your answers with the meanings given in the dictionary.

b Complete the headwords that have these meanings:

1 **pro** _ _ _ _ something difficult to answer or understand.

2 **tri** _ _ something done to deceive or fool someone.

3 **rid** _ _ _ a puzzling question, especially as a joke.

4 **sol** _ _ _ _ _ the answer to a problem or puzzle.

5 **per** _ _ _ _ to puzzle someone very much.

6 **sur** _ _ _ _ _ something that you did not expect.

7 **sus** _ _ _ _ _ _ an uncertain feeling about something.

Fill in the missing words, or parts of words, in the sentences below.
(You can use *The Oxford Primary School Dictionary* to help you.)

1 If you want a bike to run smoothly, you need to **lu** _ _ _ _ _ _ **e**

   it from time to time.

2 Deserts are **ar** _ _ places.

3 The way into the cinema is through the **fo** _ **er**.

4 Nothing was **sal** _ _ _ _ **d** from the shipwreck.

5 The number of spectators **dw** _ _ _ _ _ _ **d** to less than a dozen.

6 Detectives have to be **perc** _ _ _ _ _ _ _ in spotting clues.

7 A huge earthquake registered on the **sei** _ _ _ _ _ _ _ _ _ .

8 You can make your pocket money last longer by being more

   ec _ _ _ _ _ _ **al** with it.

9 Canoes are easy to **cap** _ _ _ _ _ .

10 How can you **jus** _ _ _ _ _ spending all that money?

11 The fireman aimed the **noz** _ _ _ at the blaze.

12 With the light behind her I could only see her **sil** _ _ _ _ _ _ _ _ .

13 The land was ruled by a cruel **ty** _ _ _ _ _ .

14 Swans have a huge **win** _ _ _ _ _ _ .

15 Security guards **pat** _ _ _ _ _ _ _ the ground regularly.

Alike – but different

Some words have very similar *meanings*. You can use a dictionary to discover how they differ.

 Say how the words in each box are alike. Then say what is different about each one.

| hill   mountain   peak   fell |

| river   stream   canal   delta |

| street   path   road   lane |

| country   county   province   district |

| fear   fright   terror   horror |

 Some words are easier to understand if you give an **example** of the way they are used:

In the entry for **spine-chilling**, which is the *meaning* and which is the *example*?

How does the dictionary show which is which?

spine-chilling *adjective*
frightening and exciting ♦ *We heard a spine-chilling ghost story*

 Think of a short example of the way these words are used:

snort   whine   roar   croak   bellow

Afterwards, look to see if your dictionary gives examples for any of these words.

....

....

....

....

....

....

You can often tell what a word means just from the words around it in a sentence – even a completely unknown word.

These sentences have been written by a visitor from another planet who is learning English. Every so often he has slipped in a word from his own language.

> Eric went to the ▼♣★▼ of the ○❻■✿✿ and looked down at the sea breaking on the jagged ✚•○❧✈ below. His mother called to him to take ○▲✚▼ but just as she ✈⑩•❧▼, the soft earth of the ○❻■✿✿ began to crumble ❧★♣▼✚ Eric's feet. He ✚▲☆ for safety.

From these clues, what do you think is the meaning of:

▼♣★▼

....

○❻■✿✿

....

✚•○❧✈

....

○▲✚▼

....

✈⑩•❧▼

....

❧★♣▼✚

....

✚▲☆

....

Write dictionary entries for some of them.

....

....

....

A job to do

'Verb', 'noun', 'adjective', 'adverb', etc. are known as

word classes or *parts of speech*

 A heavy lorry **lumbered** slowly up the hill.

The word **lumbered** tells you what the lorry did.

If you look in the dictionary you will see that the name for this kind of word is a *verb*.

lumber ➤ *verb* (**lumbers, lumbering, lumbered**)
   1 to lumber is to move along clumsily or noisily

Look up the words

lorry ....

hill ....

heavy ....

up ....

slowly ....

They are not *verbs*. What kind of words are they?

b Look in the dictionary to see what word class the names for these animals are:

monkey ....

mongoose ....

bear ....

dolphin ....

Add eight more animals to the list and write the word class beside them.

....

....

....

....

16

c Find out what part of speech words describing size and shape are:

long   **tall**   **flat**   **thin**

Think of five more to add to the list.

d Here is a list of words that tell how something might move:

quickly   **smoothly**   **awkwardly**   **backwards**

Add a few more. Which word class do these words belong to?

....

e Shaz made an **omelette**.

Shaz made a **mistake**.

Shaz made a ....

Can you think of some more nouns for things Shaz might have made? Check with the dictionary that your words are nouns.

f Colin **threw** the ball.

Colin **burst** the ball.

Colin .... the ball.

What else could Colin have done with the ball? Make as long a list as you can in *one minute*.

....

....

....

....

....

....

....

What part of speech are the words in your list?

....

17

Allsorts

Nouns are words for ***things***

thing *noun* (*plural* **things**)
an object; anything that can be touched or
seen or thought about

a Make a list of four things that you can see within a few metres of where you are. Look the words up in the dictionary and see what part of speech they are.

....

....

b Look up the words:

woman, **boy**, **sister**, **mechanic**, **athlete**

What are they all words for; and what part of speech are they?

....

....

c Here are six sets of nouns:

1 {**river, mountain, valley,** ....}

2 {**triangle, hexagon, circle,** ....}

3 {**song, ballad, tune,** ....}

4 {**heel, knee, jaw,** ....}

5 {**trawler, schooner, cruiser,** ....}

6 {**bunch, team, crowd,** ....}

Each of the nouns below also belongs to one of the six sets. Can you write them into the correct space?

gang   knuckle   square   ocean   verse   yacht

vertebra   group   ellipse   dinghy   anthem   canyon

18

 These nouns are called **proper nouns**, and they all begin with a capital letter

James   Australia   Nile   Kennedy   Paris

Say what else is different about these nouns, and think of five more examples to add to the list.

....

Are any of these words in the dictionary, and if so, where?
(Search the back of the dictionary as well as the main part).

....

....

 Nouns which are not **proper nouns** are called **common nouns**.

Complete each of these sentences with a suitable common noun from the following list: **river, country, continent, desert.**

Asia is a
....

The Amazon is a
....

The Sahara is a
....

Belgium is a
....

 A **drill** is a particular kind of **tool**.
A **sparrow** is a particular kind of **bird**.

With the help of the dictionary, find a single common noun to complete each of these sentences:

Saris, **caftans** and **kilts** are all particular kinds of ....

A **kestrel** is a particular type of ....

An **encyclopaedia** is one sort of ....

A **saxophone** is a certain kind of musical ....

A **cockroach** is an ....

19

How much? How many?

A *singular* noun stands for one thing. A *plural* noun stands for more than one.

crocodile *noun* (*plural* **crocodiles**)
  a large reptile living in hot countries, with
  a thick skin, long tail, and huge jaws

a Write down the plural form of each of these animals. Check the spelling in the dictionary, if you are unsure:

ferret   **partridge**   **goose**   **tiger**   **chaffinch**   **fox**

....

....

b The usual rule for making a noun plural is to add **-s** at the end, but this is not always how it is done.

Can you find the rule for these nouns?

glass   **dress**   **cross**   **harness**   **bus**   **crash**
branch   **bush**   **itch**   **stitch**   **watch**

....

....

c These nouns are all plural. Write down their singular forms, and say how they are all alike.

pennies   **nappies**   **parties**   **cities**   **memories**   **flies**

....

....

d Nouns ending in **-o** are the most difficult to remember.

Look up the plurals of these to find out why:

piano   **solo**   **banjo**   **flamingo**   **zoo**   **echo**
potato   **tomato**   **volcano**   **mosquito**

....

Most nouns are for things that can be counted (*countable nouns*) but some nouns have no plurals (*uncountable nouns*).

coin ➢ *noun* (*plural* **coins**)
    a piece of metal money
coin ➢ *verb* (**coins, coining, coined**)
    1 to coin money is to manufacture it
    2 to coin a new word is to invent it

You can say, "One coin, two coins, three coins, four …" **Coin** is a countable noun. But some nouns are uncountable. For example:

money *noun*
    coins and notes used by people to buy things

e Why does **money** not have a plural? Is it countable or uncountable?

....

f Which of these nouns are countable and which are uncountable? Put a 'c' by the countable nouns and a 'u' by the uncountable ones.

bread .... **loaf** .... **chair** .... **furniture** .... **spinach** ....

ocean .... **water** .... **fun** .... **game** .... **cabbage** ....

g Think of three more examples of uncountable nouns. Check their entries in the dictionary to see if they have plurals.

....

h Look up these nouns:

scissors   **trousers**   **cattle**   **shorts**

What do you notice about them?

....

i What have the plurals of these nouns got in common?
aircraft   **deer**   **sheep**

....

21

Describe it

Adjectives are words for describing things.

'There is an animal prowling round the field.'
'Is there? What kind of animal?'
'Well it's …'

 Which of the following adjectives would you have used to describe the animal on the school field? Draw a circle around the ones you have chosen.

friendly   dangerous   nasty   grotesque
cuddly   timid   captivating   inquisitive

Think of three or four more adjectives that describe the animal.

....

You could use each of these adjectives to describe different parts of the animal. Which adjective best describes each part?

jagged	....	**flickering**	....
ferocious	....	**elongated**	....
hefty	....	**clammy**	....

Colour words are adjectives. Colour the picture giving the creature a **turquoise** tail and a **crimson** neck.

b From the dictionary, find out something about these animals. Then choose a different adjective to describe each one.

eel   lizard   cheetah   sloth   weasel

....

....

....

....

....

Adjectives can be used to *compare* some things with others.

cold ➢ *adjective* (**colder**, **coldest**)
　　1 low in temperature, not hot or warm

The pool was **cold**.
The sea was **colder**.
The mountain stream was the **coldest** of all.

c Instead of the word **cold**, use the word **hard** and make up three similar sentences.

....

....

....

Make up three similar sentences comparing people or things that are:

big　fierce　angry　bad

....

....

....

d Look up these adjectives in the dictionary:

edible
flexible
disposable
inaccessible

Make up example sentences using the adjectives.

....

....

....

....

Actions

Words that describe actions belong to a large set of words called _verbs_.

Have you ever needed a dictionary in a P.E. or drama lesson? No? Well, now you do.

For the following exercises work in groups of 4–6, with at least one dictionary between you.

a Warm up by performing each of these actions in turn several times:

jump   hop   bound³   shake   wobble   slump

b Look up the following verbs in your dictionary.

lurch   jerk   slouch   flounder   glide   accept

reject   collect   possess   empty

Choose one of the words and take turns to perform the action. The others in the group have to say which one it is. Use a partner if you like.

A person (or thing) that *does* something is known as the *subject*.

c Take turns pretending that you are the subject of the following sentences. Act out what the sentence says. Then look at the questions underneath.

1   Julie tiptoed silently away from the door.

2   The animal leapt through the air with a roar.

3   The policeman arrested the burglar.

4   Carefully Lee lowered the bucket to the ground below.

Which is the verb in each sentence?

1   ....

2   ....

3   ....

4   ....

Who or what is the subject of each sentence?

1   ....

2   ....

3   ....

4   ....

d Now work out some ideas of your own.

Find an interesting or unusual verb in the dictionary. Choose a subject for it. Then make up a short sentence using the subject and the verb.

....

One or more members of your group have to act out the sentence. Carry on until everyone has had a turn.

Don't forget that more than one person or thing at a time can be a subject. For example:

*The **children** played football in their lunch hour.*

Time past

Verbs are words that have *tenses*.
Tenses are to do with time – the *past, present,* and *future.*

 a Look at the entry for the word **play**[1].

play ➤ *verb* (**plays, playing, played**)
    1 to play, or play a game, is to take part in
a game or other amusement

Which form of the verb – **play, plays, playing** or **played** – would you use to talk about the past (things that have already happened)?

b What is the past tense of each of the following verbs?

walk   jump   pick   climb

What is the rule for turning them into the past tense?

c Find the past tense of the verbs below. In what way is the spelling of the past tense of these verbs different?

skip   hop   drag   ram   propel   stir

d How do you spell the past tense of these verbs?

hurry   worry   bully   cry   reply

What is different about them?

e What about the past tense of these verbs that end in **-e**?

whine   decide   explode   care   provoke

When the past tense of a verb ends in *-d* or *-ed*, you call it a *regular* verb because it follows a rule. Many verbs are *irregular.*

f Put these verbs into the past tense, and say what you notice about them:

leap   creep   sleep   keep   dream   feel   mean
know   blow   fly   draw   throw

More about the past

Sometimes the *past* tense of a verb has its own entry in the dictionary.

wrote past tense of **write**

a   Look up these words: **ate**   **drank**   **grew**   **shrank**

What does the dictionary say about them?

b   Look up the verbs: **cooked**   **boiled**   **chopped**   **stirred**

Do they have their own entries? If not, where must you look for them?

c   Find out which of these past tense verbs have their own entries:

rose   **played**   **rang**   **drew**   **forgot**

Why do you think some are separate entries and others are not?

Some verbs have an extra form, called the *past participle*.

make ➤ *verb* (**makes, making, made**)

take *verb* (**takes, taking, took, taken**)

The past participle is for using with '**has**', '**had**', '**was**', etc.

d   Use the right forms of the verbs **make** and **take** to complete these sentences:

1   Sheena **made** a mistake: she............ the wrong train.

2   Sheena has .... a mistake: she has .... the wrong train.

e   Use the right forms of the verb **give** to complete this sentence:

I have............her the message that you .... me.

Which form is the past participle?

f   Use the dictionary to find the past tense and the past participle of each of these verbs:

eat   **wake**   **write**   **speak**   **do**

Past, Present, Future

The **present** tense is used for what is happening now, or at the time when you are speaking or writing.

> As he **crosses** the finishing line he **throws** his arms triumphantly in the air.

The **future** tense is used for what is going to happen.

> The match **will be** over in just a few minutes, and by the look of it the All-Stars **will win** the championship yet again.

The following report is written in the **past** tense. Rewrite it in the **present** tense, as though you are talking about things as they happen.

It **was** the last lap of the Italian Grand Prix and Greg, with a huge lead, **was** almost certain of victory. Suddenly, without warning one of his rear tyres **exploded**. The car **went** into a spin, and **crashed** sickeningly into the barriers. The rescue team **ran** in to assist, but thankfully the driver was already climbing out unhurt. You **could** see the anger and disappointment on his face as he **pointed** to the shattered machine.

....

....

....

....

....

....

....

....

....

....

....

....

In which tense is each of the following sentences?

1   Greg **drives** Formula One racing cars.   ....

2   Greg **will** not **drive** again this year.   ....

3   Greg **drove** a brilliant race.   ....

4   He **has driven** to victory six times.   ....

5   He**'ll be driving** again next season.   ....

29

How? When? Where?

Adverbs are words which tell us when or where or how something happens.

a yesterday   here   hurriedly   up   sometimes   easily

Which of these six adverbs say *when*?   ....

Which of them say *where* or *where to*?   ....

Which of them say *how*?   ....

b Adverbs and verbs work together in sentences. Write six sentences and in each one put one of the adverbs from **a** and one of the verbs below.

won   dressed   arrived   try   climb   wait

....

....

....

....

....

....

c Adverbs are often made by adding **-ly** to other words.

Which words do these adverbs come from? Be careful with ones that end in **-ily**.

slowly   ....

warily   ....

hungrily   ....

particularly   ....

finally   ....

30

Drama

Find the adverbs in the following sentences and look them up in your copy of
The Oxford Primary School Dictionary:

> They did the job sloppily and half-
> heartedly. The manager paid them
> reluctantly and told them not to come
> back again.

Discuss how the people behaved in these two sentences. A group of you can
work out a short play showing how they acted.

Here is a short stage direction:

> In the centre of the stage there is a
> table. On it is an envelope. Nicky
> enters, goes **immediately** to the table
> and picks up the envelope
> **inquisitively**.

Act the scene through, with one of the group as Nicky and another giving
directions.

Try changing one or both of the adverbs (**immediately** and **inquisitively**)
and then performing the scene again. You could try some of the following
adverbs, using the dictionary to help you.

indignantly   **expectantly**   **directly**   **indifferently**
defiantly   **hesitantly**   **impulsively**   **discreetly**

Discussion

Can you think of three ways in which the adverbs affect your acting?

....

....

....

Compound words

A *compound word* is made from two shorter words. For example:

nightfall = night + fall

 Here is a selection of short words. How many **compound words** can you make from them? (You can use *The Oxford Primary School Dictionary* to help you.)

green   house   boat   flood   floor   light

out   ever   hold   work   board   side

post   strong   man

You can use any word more than once.

....

....

....

....

b How many compound words can you think of that *begin* with **over-**?

....

....

....

....

When you have listed as many as you can, look in the dictionary to see how many there are there.

Can you think of some compound words that *end* with **-over**?

....

....

....

....

The game of Word Dominoes

You can use compound words to make *Word Dominoes*. Here is a game that has been started.

Can you make any new dominoes to continue the game? You can go in any direction; and you can use the dictionary to help you find new words.

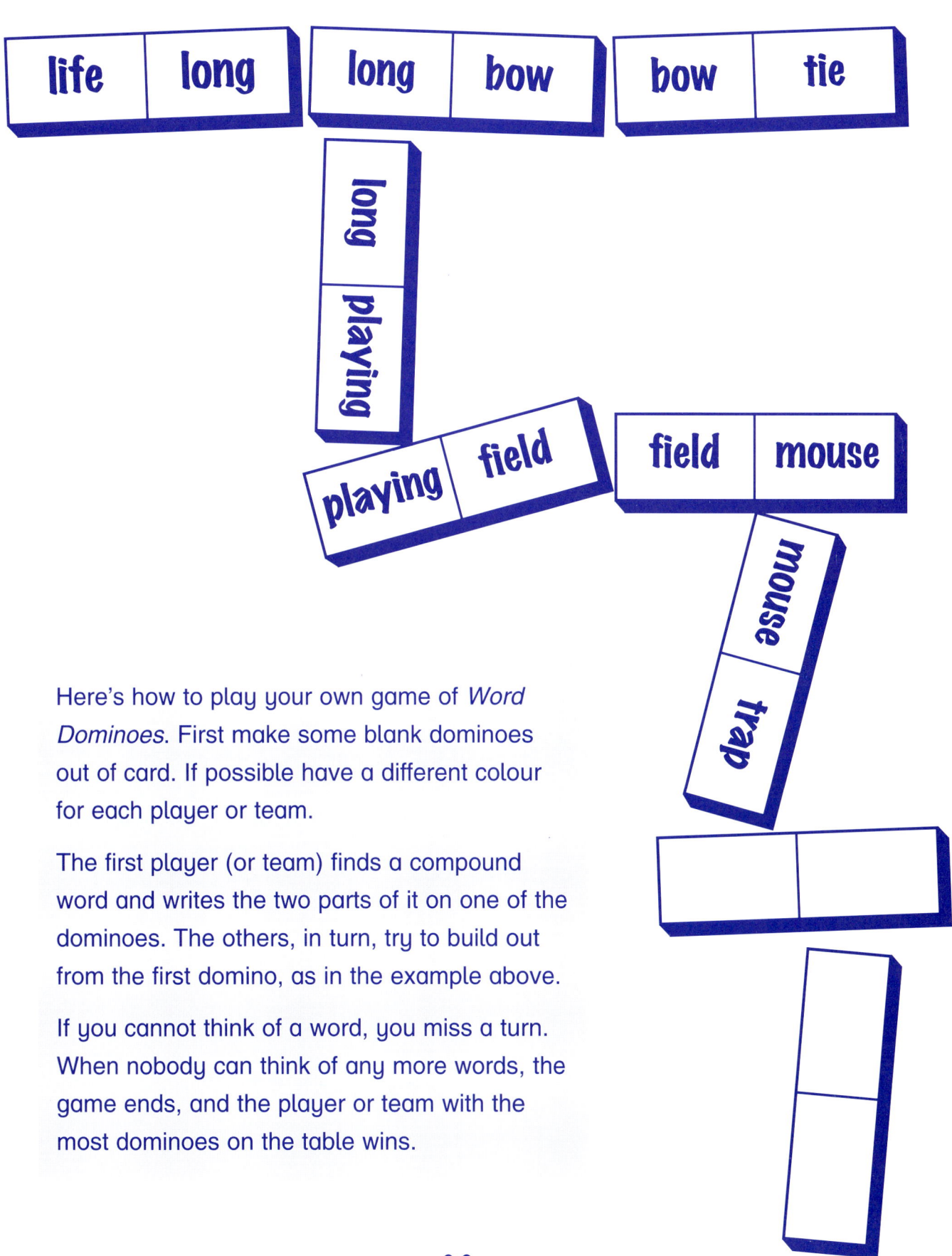

Here's how to play your own game of *Word Dominoes*. First make some blank dominoes out of card. If possible have a different colour for each player or team.

The first player (or team) finds a compound word and writes the two parts of it on one of the dominoes. The others, in turn, try to build out from the first domino, as in the example above.

If you cannot think of a word, you miss a turn. When nobody can think of any more words, the game ends, and the player or team with the most dominoes on the table wins.

All the same

The two tubes contain the same stuff. The two words *glue* and *adhesive* mean the same. Words that mean the same are called *synonyms*.

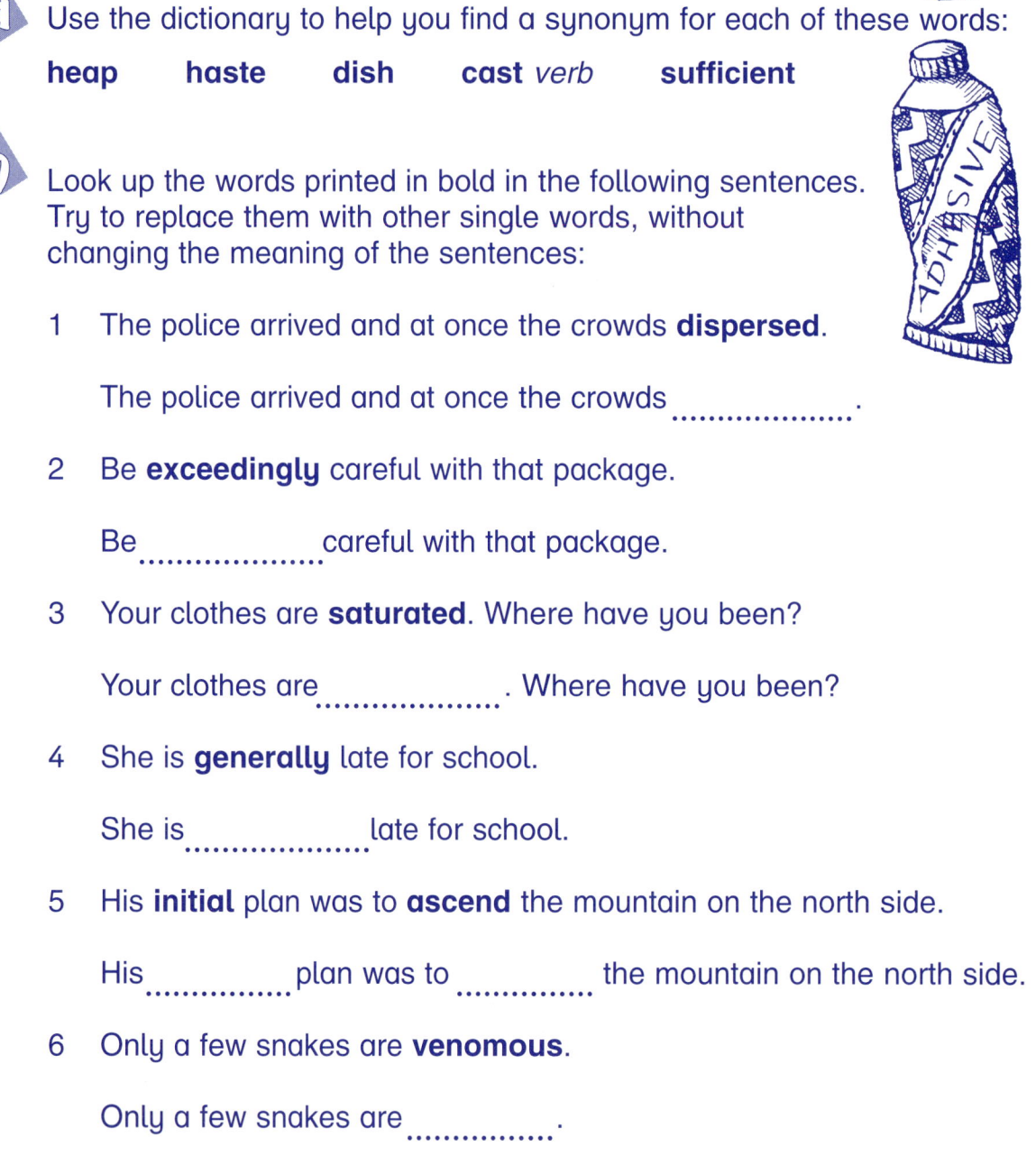

a Use the dictionary to help you find a synonym for each of these words:

heap   **haste**   **dish**   **cast** *verb*   **sufficient**

b Look up the words printed in bold in the following sentences. Try to replace them with other single words, without changing the meaning of the sentences:

1   The police arrived and at once the crowds **dispersed**.

    The police arrived and at once the crowds ....

2   Be **exceedingly** careful with that package.

    Be .... careful with that package.

3   Your clothes are **saturated**. Where have you been?

    Your clothes are .... Where have you been?

4   She is **generally** late for school.

    She is .... late for school.

5   His **initial** plan was to **ascend** the mountain on the north side.

    His .... plan was to .... the mountain on the north side.

6   Only a few snakes are **venomous**.

    Only a few snakes are ....

Discussion

Can you think why there are sometimes two or more words with the same meaning?

Is it *useful* to have two or more words that mean the same? If so, why?

The game of Synonyms

Here are 15 pairs of words that mean the same as each other – only they are all mixed up.

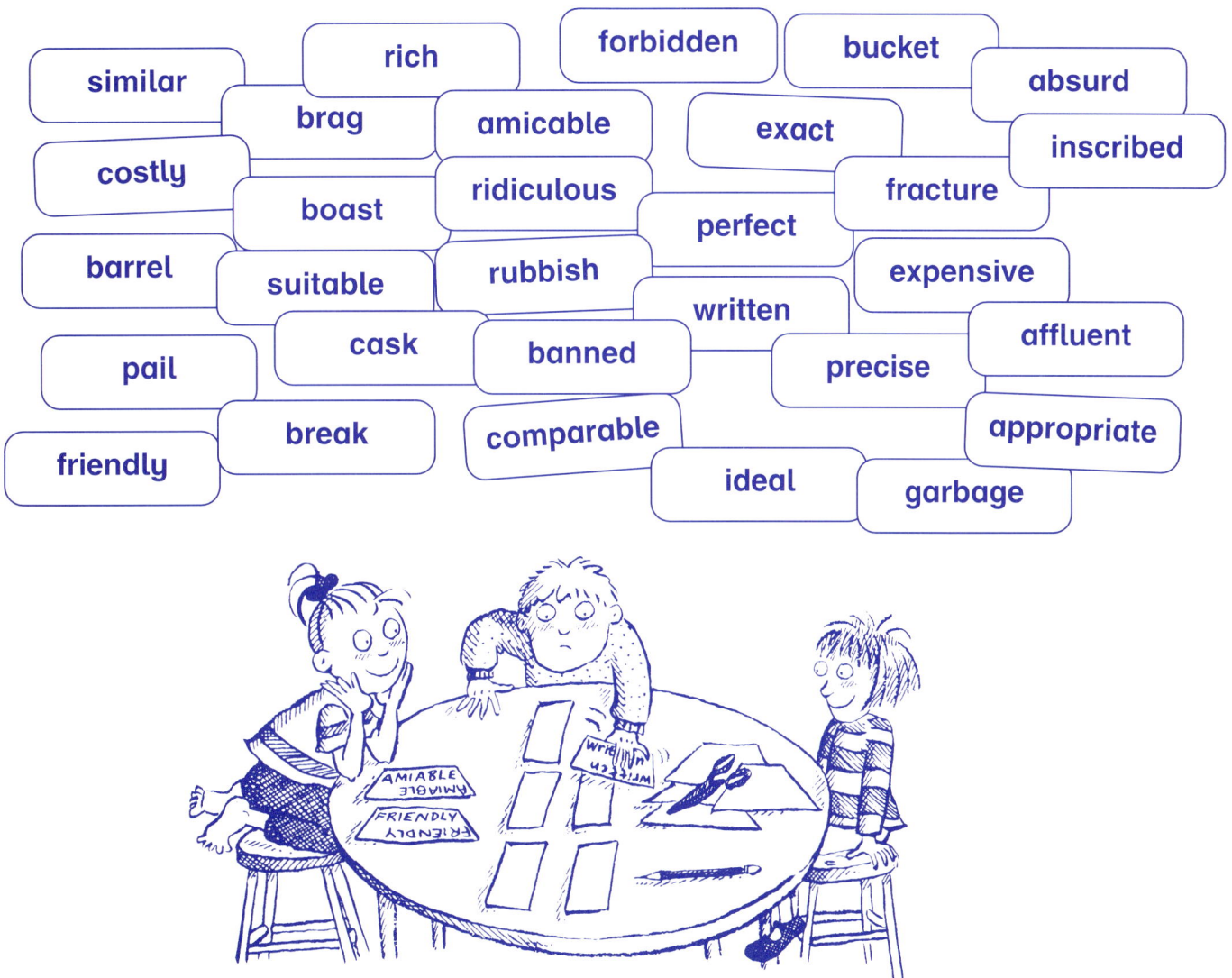

Write each word on a card and place all the cards face down on a table.

Take turns to turn over two cards so that everyone can see them. If they mean the same thing, keep them and have another go straight away. If they do not mean the same thing, turn them face down again and your turn ends.

The player who ends up with the most pairs, wins.

You can use *The Oxford Primary School Dictionary* to look up the words before and during this game.

Opposites

These pairs of words mean the **opposite** of each other.

>   high, low
>   wet, dry
>   difficult, easy

a Think of an opposite for each of these words:

top   ....

long   ....

loud   ....

rapid   ....

front   ....

b Look these up in the dictionary and then think of a word that is the opposite of each one:

fragrant   ....

fruitless   ....

genuine   ....

remote   ....

casual   ....

occasional ....

c A lot of words can be made to mean the opposite by adding one of these to the beginning:

>   un-
>   in-
>   im-
>   il-
>   ir-
>   anti-

They are called **prefixes.**

Choose the correct prefix for each of these words to turn them into their opposites. Try each in turn until you find a dictionary entry for each opposite.

possible   ....

legal   ....

necessary   ....

secure   ....

responsible ....

clockwise   ....

d Make these sentences mean the opposite by changing one or more words in each of them.

The accident was unavoidable.

....

The children behaved in a very immature way.

....

Colin's writing is illegible.

....

He was an unkind and intolerant man.

....

The drummer beat a loud and irregular rhythm.

....

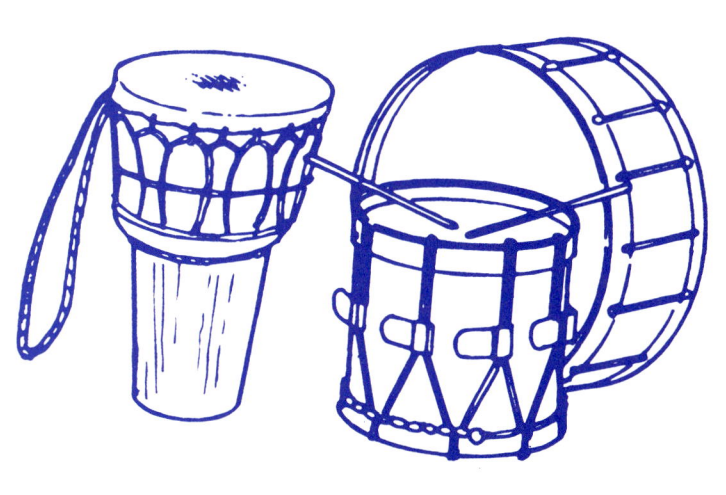

Shopping

 Look up the words for these shops and then make a short list of some of the things you could buy in each one:

newsagent   **delicatessen**   **boutique**   **greengrocer**

....

....

....

Which of the following would you find in a **hardware** shop?

lentils   **brackets**   **washers**   **swedes**

....

Supermarkets have signs above the shelves to help you find the things you want.

Look at the picture opposite. Copy it and write the names of these goods on the shelves where they belong:

courgettes   oatmeal   muesli   yoghurt

swedes   yams   cream   spinach   Cheddar

 Look at the table below.

Across the top are shops. Down the side are the first letters of goods you can buy in these shops. For example:

plug begins with **p** and a **plug** is **electrical**

electrical shop	clothes shop	food shop
plug	p	p
r	r	r
b	b	b
t	t	t
w	w	w

To complete the table you have to put one correct *noun* in each box. See how many you can find, using the dictionary to help you.

Try making a similar table with different shops and different letters. You can make your own game out of completing the table. Decide on rules before you begin. (For example, you could give an extra point for any word no one else in your group has thought of.)

Crossword

Clues

The first letter of each answer is given to you.

Across

1 *verb* to keep someone or something safe

7 *adjective* ready to be harvested or eaten

8 *noun* a mixture of smoke and fog

9 *noun* what you can see from one place

10 *noun* a circle

12 *noun* a person who does gymnastics

Down

2 *noun* a small, soft, red, fruit

3 *verb* to pull something along behind you

4 *noun* the best people in sports, competitions, etc.

5 *noun* a small house on wheels

6 *adjective* having promised to marry someone

11 *verb* past tense of **win**

Here are some more clues. See if you can work them out:

A   A car can [3 down] a [5 down].

B   People often wear a [10 across] when they are [6 down].

C   You should not eat a [2 down] until it is [7 across].

D   [8 across] can spoil the [9 across].

Little and large

a All of these are young animals. What would their parents be?

goslings .... **fawns** .... **foals** ....

cygnets .... **lambs** ....

Name four animals whose young ones are called cubs:

....

....

b What do the following become when they are fully grown? An asterisk*
means that more than one answer is possible.

seedlings ....

tadpoles* ....

kids* ....

acorns ....

calves* ....

c Each of the eight words below is a small *something*: a small what?

dinghy .... **chuckle** .... **snack** ....

ripple .... **nap** .... **chapel** .... **brook** ....

d These are all words for parts of an army. Look them up and write them
down in order, with the largest one at the top.

company ....

brigade ....

platoon ....

battalion ....

division ....

42

e What are these?

a **piglet** ....

a **booklet** ....

a **minibus** ....

f Put these *adjectives* into order, starting with the one meaning largest:

minute sizeable microscopic immense infinite small

....

....

g There are two sets of words below, all mixed up. Five of them describe light and five describe sound. Can you make them into two lists, with the strongest at the top and the weakest at the bottom?

**loud   dim   soft   brilliant   thunderous   inaudible
bright   deafening   dazzling   invisible**

....

....

....

....

....

h Sometimes people make up words for small things. Just for fun, try making up a word for each of these. Put the plurals in the brackets.

noun (....)
     a small street with houses on both sides.

noun (....)
     a very short lesson on a Friday afternoon.

noun (....)
     a small piece of chocolate broken off a big
     bar, by someone who is not very generous.

Whose suggestions do you think are the best? Whose are funniest?

43

Shape and space

 a Label the shapes, giving them their correct names.

**cone   cylinder   cuboid   semicircle
parallelogram   pentagon
prism**

b Draw a **set-square** and say what it is used for.

....

....

....

....

c What is the **radius** of a circle?

You can answer in words, or by drawing in the box.

....

....

....

....

d List three things that are sphere-shaped.

....

....

....

e Which is the larger area: a **hectare** or an **acre**?

....

f Label these angles correctly, using the words **acute** and **obtuse**

120⁰   60⁰

g

This shape is a *hel* _ _ .

This is an *isos* _ _ _ _ _ triangle.

Draw an **ellipse**.

Draw a shape that **tapers** at one end.

Draw an insect that has a **symmetrical** shape.

Where does it come from?

All words have a story behind them; some are more interesting than others. Most of our words come from the Old English language; or from Norse that the Vikings spoke; or from the French that came over with William the Conqueror. Many go further back to Latin or Greek. And today words continue to come into English from all corners of the world.

WORD ORIGIN means where a word came from, and what it once meant. You will find many entries in *The Oxford Primary School Dictionary* which give word origins. They look like this:

sherbet *noun* (*plural* **sherbets**)
a fizzy sweet powder or drink

i WORD ORIGIN
The word **sherbet** comes from an Arabic word *sharbat* meaning 'a drink'

 Use this table to give the origins of the words in the first column

English word	Language of Origin	Old word	Old meaning
e.g. sherbet	*Arabic*	*sharabat*	*drink*
admiral			
meteor			
fort			
cagoule			

2 Some word origins are easy to guess. You only have to look at them. Try these, then check in the dictionary to see if you were right:

holiday   deckchair   nightmare   horsepower   towpath   steamroller

 But some are more surprising. Try guessing the origins of these words before you look them up. Then write the correct origins beside them.

see-saw ....

deadline ....

red herring ....

turncoat ....

checkmate ....

barbecue ....

 This table has English words on the left and languages of origin on the right, but they are not matched up. Draw a line joining each word to its language of origin, like the one showing that **emu** came from Portuguese.

camouflage	**German**
barracks	**Italian**
spell	**Old English**
emu	**French**
galore	**Latin**
temple	**Japanese**
hero	**Spanish**
souvenir	**Greek**
delicatessen	**Portuguese**
racket	**Irish**
origami	**Arabic**

 Who or Where?
Some of these words (or phrases) come from the names of places and some from the names of people:

**guinea   braille   jersey
magnolia   mackintosh
Morse Code   tangerine
turkey   pasteurised
newtons   watts   muslin**

Sort the words into two sets using the blank table:

Places	People

 There is a unusual connection between **pal** and *brother*.
Find out what it is. Then find words from the list below that are connected with the other words in the table. Write them in the spaces.

arrow   head   garden   thunder   rivers

pal	upshot	paradise	poll	tornado	rivals
brother					

A lively activity book, designed to motivate children to use **The Oxford Primary School Dictionary** and develop early reference skills.

Using
The
OXFORD
Primary School Dictionary

► Provides games, exercises, quizzes, and puzzles for individuals and groups

► Encourages children to use a dictionary across the school curriculum

► Stimulates an interest in language

► Extends vocabulary, aids spelling, and improves comprehension

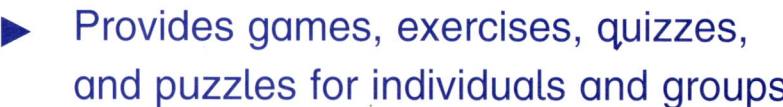

Also available:
The Oxford Primary School Dictionary
Written with the help of teachers and tested in schools, this new dictionary will improve vocabulary, answer queries on written and spoken English, and encourage children to learn about language.

The
OXFORD
Primary School Dictionary

► *Help with spelling and grammar*
► *Over 24,000 headwords*
► *Illustrated throughout*

NEW EDITION

For children of eight upwards.

Orders and enquiries to
Customer Services:
Tel: 01536 741171
Fax: 01536 454519

ISBN 0-19-910455-7

9 780199 104550